Growing Up Country
AND LIKING IT!

Grace Ollis Calhoun
Jean Ollis Honeycutt
Jessie Shields Strickland

The Overmountain Press

JOHNSON CITY, TENNESSEE

ISBN 1-57072-035-5

1 2 3 4 5 6 7 8 9 0

For Jenna, Amber, Jeremy, Andrea, and Nancy.
Part of your legacy lies within these pages—we love you!

TABLE OF CONTENTS

INTRODUCTION

In the late 1800s and early 1900s, Cranberry, a small rural community in Western North Carolina, was a booming iron ore mining town. The Cranberry Iron Ore Mines had supported a thriving community, as is evidenced by the company row houses which were built along the main thoroughfare. A theater, swimming pool, ballpark, and country store were at the hub of the community's prosperity. But the railroad left and, like many other Appalachian communities, the iron ore mines folded. However, Cranberry was still home to many and provided a strong kinship to the mountain people. The community members remaining after the closure of the iron ore mines turned to each other for support. Strong ties during hard times made family and friends inseparable, and a sense of humor emerged for most.

Valley Forge, a small community of Carter County near Elizabethton, Tennessee, got its name from the iron industry which flourished before the Civil War. Valley Forge had a natural beauty of its own. Doe River flowed—and still does—through a natural gap between the Iron and Jenkins mountains and wound northward through Elizabethton to join with the Watauga River. In the pioneer days one of the main routes to North Carolina was through this gap. Tradition says the frontiersmen took this route on their way to King's Mountain to defeat the British army in 1780. Valley Forge inhabitants are proud of their history and tradition. Growing up in this close-knit community was a kind experience. Everyone seemed to know everyone else, many were kin, and most cared about each other.

— COMMON FACTS ABOUT COUNTRY FOLKS —

Most older people in the Appalachians are commonly referred to as "Uncle" or "Aunt," whether kin or not; in general most are kin.

Republicans and Baptists were one and the same in Cranberry for the most part. Valley Forge was home for mostly

Republicans, too; however, Methodist and Christian churches were there with the Baptist ones, as well.

Church was the focal point for socialization. If you could sing or play an instrument—and most could—and were Baptist and Republican, you could be classified as a churchgoing member. Sister or Brother introducing a name—i.e., Brother Emmett, Sister Hattie—generally meant the mountain person was definitely a churchgoer.

Banana pudding was dubbed "funeral pudding" because of its frequency in being brought to the residence of a family in mourning. It was—and is now—mountain etiquette to take food to the family of the dearly departed. Also, mountain cooking is still visible at most church functions and at happy or sad occasions. Instead of saying, "Let's drink to that," mountain people say, "Let's eat to that." We'll eat most anything, anytime!

Most everyone in the Western North Carolina and East Tennessee area was given a nickname. Such nicknames as "Junior," "Lum," "Tootie," "Pink," "Tump," "Hutch," "Slim," "Babe," "Duck," "Poke," "Pig," "Catman," "Chub," and "Jug" were commonplace. The quickest way to give away your unfamiliarity with an area was to use the birth name of a mountain person, for doing so denoted a "fereigner" (foreigner) to the area. If a child did not have a nickname, the full name was used. Examples are Sammy Joe, Lois Ann, Billy Jack, John Jay, Peggy Sue, and Ray Lacey.

ABOUT THE AUTHORS

Grace Ollis Calhoun is the Superintendent of Cobb County Schools, Marietta, Georgia. She has degrees from Gardner Webb College, Boiling Springs, North Carolina; Mercer University, Macon, Georgia; and West Georgia College. She lives in Marietta with her husband, Doyle. She is the mother of two daughters, Nancy and Andrea.

Grace has received many awards, most recently Germany's highest, the Federal Republic of Germany Friendship Award, and an award from the Catholic church for conducting cultural diversity classes. She is president of Metro Superintendents in Atlanta and was elected vice chair of the Control Board for Metropolitan Regional Educational Services Agency.

Grace's childhood memories of Cranberry, North Carolina, are fond. She was the soprano for the Cranberry Girls' Quartet, and she sang and played the piano and guitar.

Grace speaks throughout the South to varied audiences about her mountain raising, for which she is proud. Her rich mountain heritage, culture, and folklore experiences are embedded in her vivacious personality. Coworkers, family, and friends enjoy her mountain preaching monologues.

Jean Ollis Honeycutt, a sister to Grace Ollis Calhoun and one of ten children born to Brown and Bertha Ollis, attended Lees-McRae College, Banner Elk, North Carolina. She is an Accredited Medical Record Technician. She has a teaching husband, Gene, and two children: Amber, a junior at Carson-Newman College, Jefferson City, Tennessee, and Jeremy, a freshman at East  Tennessee State University, Johnson City, Tennessee. The Honeycutt family lives in Johnson City.

Jean, still musically active in her church, learned to play the piano by ear at the age of nine. She lived with her mother after the death of her and Grace's father. The time Jean spent with her mother bonded them further, and she can recall many anecdotes her mother shared.

Jean is presently an Administrative Assistant to the Superintendent of the Elizabethton City School System, Elizabethton, Tennessee. Her family remains her lifeblood, and in the Honeycutt home, mountain anecdote telling for her family and friends has become a standard part of leisure time activities.

A loving mother, father, and nine brothers and sisters served as inspirations for Grace and Jean to "make it in life."

Jessie Shields Strickland, one of five children born to Samuel and Lena Pearman Shields, has childhood memories from farm life in Cripple Creek, Virginia, to rural life at Valley Forge, a suburb of Elizabethton, Tennessee. Jessie's mother has held the key to unlock the fondest of growing up years. Mrs. Shields raised the children on her own after Mr.  Shields died at age forty-two and near Jessie's fifth birthday.

Jessie is the Superintendent of the Elizabethton City Schools. She has been an educator since nineteen years of age and has twenty-four years of experience combining teaching and school supervision. She served as the Language Arts Specialist for Tennessee's State Department of Education for five years.

She has authored numerous professional materials, work texts, and programs, including a vocational education student work text, *English for the VIP's*, used in thirteen states; a statewide Language Arts diagnostic prescriptive individualized computer managed program, *Project Manage*; and a Tennessee history book, *Horizons of Tennessee*. Jessie was a consulting author for five California history books and was twice the featured writer for *Blue Ridge Country* magazine. She has B.S., M.A., and Ed.D. degrees from East Tennessee State University in Johnson City, Tennessee.

She lives on Powder Branch in Johnson City with her husband, Robert, Assistant Director of ETSU Physical Plant, and daughter, Virginia Elizabeth ("Jenna"), a fifth grader at West Side School in Elizabethton. The family values their time together making memories for Jenna.

**Cranberry General Store
Post Office to left, 1950s**

The Grocery Store—The Hub
of Country Survival

Cranberry

My childhood memories of the one large grocery store in Cranberry, Pop's General Merchandise, are fond ones. On any given hot summer day, my main mission in life was to take that daily half-mile walk down to Pop's General Merchandise for whatever reason—to buy a Pepsi-Cola for five cents (My sister Alberta said I would swap my seat in Heaven for a Pepsi-Cola when I was a child! She also told me how she and my other sister, Ludella, would drink the Pepsi down about three-fourths of the way, then add water to make it last longer. They would have enough to give the younger brothers and sisters a "swig"!); to buy a tin of Bruton's Dental Sweet Snuff for Great Aunt Lessie, who lived next to me; or to select the print of a sack of chop feed for the cow. This would later be delivered by Pop, the owner; or Bob and Joe, my brothers, would take it home on their Mercury red wagon. The fifty-pound bags of chop feed came in different colored printed cloth sacks that Mama used to make our dresses, underwear, pillow cases, and table spreads. Choosing a "pretty" sack of chop feed was definitely in the eyes of the beholder, since one could chance going to school and facing the girl in the next aisle with a dress just like yours! The colorful print material sure did beat the underwear that was made from the white chop sacks with the hog's head on them!

Our groceries were "charged," "set-up," or "put on account" from month to month. Then one day a month, when Mama paid the grocery bill, we all waited anxiously for her return from the store. Pop always sent us a brown bag filled with loose, mixed candy. I would eat so much of it (after fighting my brother Bob for it) that by nightfall I was usually so hyper Mama would wind up spanking me and putting me to bed early. The only kind I didn't like was the wax orange slices. I loved, however, the orange marshmallow peanuts.

The general store was the main hub of the community, especially since the post office was located directly beside it, with only a partition separating the two. Everyone would flock to the store and wait for the mailman to bring the mail. It was an exciting and challenging time when the post office got boxes with combination locks. Prior to that you just asked for your mail. Not everyone learned to open the boxes, and some continued to "ask" for their mail always.

Most days, even in the summertime because the store was so big and drafty, the potbellied stove would be going. Everyone had to gather around it close to get a faint draft of heat every now and then. The men would sit behind the stove and play checkers, smoke, swig on Coca-Colas, and tell tall tales. The women would browse the store wishing for things they could not afford, like two yards of the beautiful bolted material on the shelf instead of a chop sack to make a dress. The young boys would wait anxiously by their dads' sides around the stove, calling for "ducks" or "dubs" on the Cokes. The men would leave one good swallow in the bottom of the Coke bottle for the young boys, who would "down" it as fast as lightning.

When the mail truck arrived, everyone would look to see who was in the truck. There were few cars or trucks in Cranberry, so people rode the mail truck from one post office to another to conduct their business and wait for the truck's return in the afternoon to go back home. The mailman graciously hauled anyone and everyone he could. He had installed side benches in the back of the covered truck to haul passengers.

Pop's General Merchandise was our voting site on election day. I couldn't wait to give out campaign cards for someone running for office, because that meant I would get a free Pepsi-Cola at the end of the day. If I was lucky, I might get a cheese sandwich or bologna sandwich also for a nickel. There were no fast-food places or restaurants. There was only one snack bar, and it was too far to walk. The country store served as the only fast-food place. Sandwiches there were made from real "light" bread—not wheat biscuits or pone bread!

The grocery store also served as our "health clinic." The county health nurse and doctor would come to the store to check us and give us our shots (childhood immunizations). That's the only time I ever tried to get out of going to the store. Mama would announce that the health nurse would be coming on the next Tuesday to give shots, and I would lay awake at night as a child and pray for the nurse to die before the next Tuesday. Much to my dismay, when Tuesday rolled around, Mama would herd us all together, and down to the store we'd go, my legs shaking a little harder with each step.

After the misery was over, Mama would say, "Now, that wasn't so bad, was it?"

I'd always say, "Yes, it was, Mama, and you know it!" Then she'd take me in her arms and console me. Deep down, I'd sigh a sigh of relief knowing the immunization ordeal was over until the next summer.

When I was about six years old, our neighbor, Mr. Will, got a 1950 black Chevrolet. (He was one of the few men in Cranberry to have a car of any kind at that time.) We were all overjoyed when Mr. Will would stop and drive my mama and daddy to church, or when he would stop by our house and pick up my daddy to go to the store and post office each day. On warm summer days, Daddy would be sitting on the front porch waiting for Mr. Will to come by and pick him up. My brothers and sisters and I would beg Daddy to let us ride with him in the back of the car. There was no back seat, just an area we could crawl in and ride. We didn't care. We would have stood on the running board and ridden if Daddy would have allowed it. Anything to get to ride in a car!

Pop's General Merchandise is gone now, but a flood of memories still remains, and in those memories it's still there and still just the same—the same potbellied stove, the same oiled hardwood floors, the same merchandise, and the same loving people.

Valley Forge

The country store at Valley Forge was not much different in use than Pop's General Merchandise in Cranberry. It was *the* place to go for purchasing most everything. The local old-timers sat across the outside front in the heat of summer and moved inside around the old potbellied stove in late October. The men always seemed to be drinking Dr. Enuf, a carbonated drink which professed to have the enrichments of vitamins and minerals along with a huge amount of caffeine. I can safely say I never saw a female with a Dr. Enuf in her hand. It was sorta the unspoken drink of men back then, and a girl didn't ever tread over to the Enuf side of the Coca-Cola floor case where all the "pops" were bottleneck high in cold water. Dr. Enufs served a dual-purpose role. They were the drink of real men who used the empty bottles as spittoons when chewing their Bull of the Woods, Day's Work, Brown Mule, or Apple tobacco.

Merchandising to Edith, the short, plump, and kind store owner, simply meant getting as much as she could get on the shelves, floor, and in the showcases. Christmastime was extra special at the Valley Forge store. I couldn't wait to go with Mama to settle-up our monthly account during this holiday. Edith would always total all those carbon-backed pieces of paper on her crank-handled adding machine, move around to the right front of the store, and proceed to fill a large plain brown grocery bag with "treats." At Christmas, Mama's brown bag always held a half-gallon of Neapolitan

Pet ice cream. Since there were five of us kids, Edith knew all would be satisfied, because the Neapolitan had something for everyone—chocolate, strawberry, and vanilla layers.

Edith would toddle over to the large Christmas assortment of bagged candies, which sat beneath the left side of the store's window. There she had half-pint-sized bags, and she'd fill each with old-fashioned chocolate drops, assorted coconut haystacks, and orange slices; and lastly she would put in stick candy, mostly peppermint. Only once did she slip a couple sticks of horehound in on us—it was a catastrophe. We kids wanted to boycott her for that one slip! When Edith was in a generous mood, and Mama's bill had been a big one for the month, like the time it was $21.00 (the first month Edith started merchandising "push-up" ice creams, cinnamon-colored hosiery, boxed get-well cards, and Bunny bread in the same month), she would throw in a box of chocolate-covered cherries and a pair of socks for each of us.

Edith liked my mama. My mama would frequently cook a tray of hot food and carry it all the way to the store to her, about a half mile. I believe most everyone held my mama in high esteem because she was a widow-lady. My daddy had died suddenly of a heart attack when I was five years old. That left my mama with five children to raise—a three year old, a five year old, a six year old, a ten year old, and a thirteen year old. We were treated with great care by our neighbors, and Edith and her husband, Clyde, were no exceptions. Their country store was just as much a part of my childhood as were my three sisters and brother.

My sisters and I would much rather face Edith than Clyde during the crisis of what we called "entry into womanhood." It was so embarrassing to have to tell Clyde what you wanted. My "entry into womanhood" experience came all too soon for me. Sure enough, I had to deal with Clyde.

The "monthlies," "grannies," "that time again," "the misery," and "started" characterize a few of the country names attached to the monthly menstrual cycle. The thing was that you never remembered hearing about the monthlies until it smack-dab happened to you. Age varied, but the monthlies struck every female sooner or later. It was nature's ritual for calling us females into womanhood. It was a mama's, older sister's, or bosom buddy's ritual to explain it.

The monthlies usually showed up at the most inconvenient times—like your first date or on swimming pool or swimming hole day—or it could just crawl up on you like it did me, the first day of sixth grade. Nature didn't call me during the school day, thank goodness, like it had Nanny Lovelace, who everybody knew had a problem when she had to go to the blackboard and her green 4-H skirt had a really big red splotch on the back of it. Mrs. West took her to the bathroom, post haste—but we all knew something was up. Most of the boys thought she cut herself on the splintered wooden desk which came over on Noah's Ark. Some of the girls thought Nanny was bleeding to death from some ill-fallen disease caught at school in Mrs. West's class. Most other girls were a little more clever. They knew Nanny was to never be the same from that day forward. She'd get the "talk" about how you are a woman now and have to keep your drawers on at all times or the stork comes a-calling and the family's disgraced and you've "ruint" your life forever.

No, I was spared the two safety pins and pad at public school, unlike poor Nanny. A girl going into womanhood ought to be at least in privacy to have her first monthly.

My monthly happened as I tuned into *Yancey Darringer* on our black and white, twelve-inch, plastic-encased, portable TV. It had been my first day in sixth grade, and my nerves needed to be calmed from all that rote and drill instruction that comes with the first day of school. Also, sixth grade began life in the social lane for many girls—which meant you got answers, mostly a check, in the right box from your boyfriend. Up to now, boys kind of ignored "Do you love me, *yes* or *no*." I was drained from my first day, and thirty minutes with Yancey in my favorite TV chair, with a third of a bottle of Grapette gulped down. (I'm pretty sure I only got a third of the Grapette, 'cause two of my sisters and I passed the bottle back and forth during TV time, and we were pretty fair about the size of each swig we took from the bottle.) As I sat there totally enthralled in Yancey and the Grapette, my older sister, who was a woman and had been one for a year unbeknownst to me, must have seen my drawers when I got up to hand her the bottle of Grapette. She "ecked" and yelled for Mama. They went into the kitchen, whispering while staring at me like I had the plague.

In less than five minutes, I was given the "talk" and sent up the hill on foot to the grocery store with a note penciled on the torn corner of a brown paper bag. Mercy! I was going to have to get my own pads. I guess womanhood meant more responsibility, too. I wasn't much liking becoming a woman. I didn't know how to get out of it; after all, Mama had said it was "something that afflicted all girls." The way I saw it, I was now afflicted for good, and no turning back without those pads.

It was no surprise to me either that the co-owner and brains of the grocery store, Edith, had gone home already. I had to give my note to Clyde, her husband. Now Clyde was as good as gold. He was a man of few words and had been left a crippled hand from polio. I always did my yellow and green Tom's and Teaberry gum buying from Edith. I just couldn't ever quit gazing at Clyde's withered hand when he came toward me, so I felt it was better to transact candy and gum business with Edith.

Today was the exception. It would be Clyde who would read my brown bag note which had been written by my mom with Edith in mind..."Dear Edith, little Duckie is a woman today. Please give her a box of pads. Thank you, Mrs. Shields."

Mercy! I held out as long as I could. Edith was definitely not coming back. Clyde was growing impatient. After all, he and three locals, the grocery usuals—Herb, Cart, and Harve—were conversationally engaged around the back of the grocery store, even though there wasn't a fire. Clyde wanted me to conduct my business and be gone. It seemed hours, but I reckon I finally decided there's just so much Ajax, Spic and Span, Clorox, and Borax a girl can look at. I handed him my note. I truly liked Clyde better at that very moment. He read it, nodded understandingly, and walked to the back behind his cronies and began to retrieve my pads.

In grocery stores in the early '50s, pads were kept in the most discreet place ever thought possible. Clyde's work was cut out for him. He got a long fishing rod-looking pole and with his withered hand began to poke at the boxes of pads which appeared to be at least ten feet high on the shelves. The three men around the stove must have known my predicament, and they showed respect—quiet as church mice.

Clyde was having difficulty with something among the boxes, which had a red stripe or a green stripe on the front. Finally, this quiet grocer yelled at me. I was standing as far away from the activity in the back as one could in a country grocery store. Clyde boomed, "You want ragular or extree large?"

With face red with humiliation, I cast my eyes to the oiled plank floor and managed to squeak out, "The little ones, please, Clyde." In a flash, Clyde went for the red striped box, and just for a second I feared Clyde had met his doom, 'cause the fishing rod-like pole had unearthed box after box of red and green striped sanitary pad boxes, and all came tumbling down on him as well as on Herb, Cart, and Harve.

I knew right then and there my mama didn't have to be worried about "someone getting into my drawers." Her biggest worry was going to be ever getting me to go in that grocery store again. My entry into womanhood was forever etched in my memory.

Years later, when sanitary napkins were on shelves visible to the public, one ol' gentleman who was the town's most "slow learner" asked what was in the large blue box marked "Kotex." Clyde answered, "Radio batteries," because he knew he would never be able to explain to the fellow what it really was. All us girls tuned in monthly to the radio and bought many batteries!

Church Going—All About the Flock and the Preachers

Church going to most mountain folks was looked upon with utmost importance. First, we considered ourselves God-fearing; and second, the only place to go see everybody in the community and to catch up on the local news was church. Mostly, we Appalachians were Baptist, some Holiness, some Church of Christ, and a few Methodist and Presbyterian. My local church was a Union church for years, which meant every denomination had a turn at peppering their doctrine down your throat on their Sunday to preach. Traveling preachers, who went from church to church, visited my church often. But the one common thread through all the practicing denominations was the unity among the members and the family-like atmosphere of the church. The preacher was often one of the most influential members of the community, second only to the teacher.

Cranberry

Preachers added local color to our growing up. Their personalities were as different as day and night. During the years of the Union Church, one particular traveling preacher, who was very committed to serving the Lord, was also one of the most interesting preachers. He was a lean, towering man whose legs seemed to go on forever. He prided himself in his immaculate dress and his slow, distinctly pronounced speech.

He began on a Wednesday night's prayer meeting, "Friends, tonight let's be pacific [specific] about this," or at the end of his most sincere sermon, "Let this be a lecture [lesson] unto us." A classic incident occurred when he attended a local Saturday night singing in the community. We were all singing and enjoying ourselves. Each song sung met with the preacher's "Amen." Being the considerate person he was, he faithfully complimented each singer during the conversation that would occur between songs. After a while, he realized he had not complimented the talented pianist. Acting quickly to rectify the situation, the preacher sat with his back as straight as an arrow, leaned forward with his head mechanically moving up and down, and said, "I'll tell you one thing, I do believe Sister Mary is about the best penis [pianist] I've ever seen!" Needless to say, we all lost our composure!

Another preacher who was fondly revered in the community was an elderly, white-haired minister who was also a traveling circuit-riding minister. He boarded Friday night until Monday morning with my family each week. He was a well-educated man and never met a stranger. His personality beamed, and he was always happy and upbeat.

He was known for his visits to those who attended church, as well as to those who were not among the flock. He worked diligently at adding members to his flock and taking care of them.

He tipped his hat to all he met. "Top of the morning," he'd say. Saturdays seemed to be his best day to get the local girls' quartet together. We girls—my sister Brownell was also a member—always accompanied him on his visits. One Saturday in particular, the preacher felt called to visit an elderly couple in the community who were in ill health. Although neither was a member of his congregation, the preacher counted them as part of his flock.

As the quartet followed six paces behind the preacher, they met the elderly man face to face at his front door. "Top of the morning, top of the morning," greeted the preacher with his hat in hand. "I've carried the girls to sing for you today, Brother Haskiel."

And to that, Brother Haskiel, in his gruffest voice, retorted, "They'll be no sanging today. Maw's got to mop!"

Another preacher who brought colorful memories to our community was a seventy-year-old, tall, lanky man with long strands of straight white hair combed over his balding head. He wore suspenders and arm garters which could be seen on his long-sleeved shirts when he removed his coat to preach. He would occasionally peer over his thick spectacles when speaking.

One Sunday morning in the early '50s, he ascended the steps to the rostrum, laid down his huge Bible, opened it to the middle, pulled the spectacles down on his nose, and peered over the audience. He pulled back the coat of his suit, placed his fingers in his suspenders, and began to flex them while rocking back and forth. He stared intently over the audience, which seemed to go forever. He then began, "Dear folk, today I'm going to read you a little Palm [Psalm]. This Palm is one which is knowed by all of us. This Palm is one we've cited many a time. This, my dear fold, is the Twenty-third Palm." He loved the sermon he preached on the Twenty-third "Palm" almost as well as his favorite sermon on the "Alabaster Box." He preached about it at least once every three months.

One interesting mountain preacher was a constant talker. He was always on the go, good-natured, and easygoing. In the early '40s, the only means of public transportation to any town in the Appalachian mountains was by the Queen City Trailways bus. The bus ran a daily route from Elk Park to Asheville, North Carolina, and back. Many people from Cranberry rode the bus daily to Plumtree to work in the Tar Heel Mica plant. The Queen City busses of the '40s were not equipped with bathroom facilities. This mountain preacher was a regular rider on the bus going to Plumtree each day. The bus would make stops anywhere along the route. The rider would reach up and pull a cord which sounded above the window and signaled to the driver that someone wanted off the bus. One particular day when the preacher was on the bus, he pulled the cord and signaled the driver to stop the bus. There were no houses around, and everyone wondered why he wanted off the bus in such a sparsely populated area. The preacher ran down the aisle of the bus, unfastening his pants, and shouted to the driver, "Shut her down, Pard! I'm a busting!"

The driver opened the door, and the preacher leaped off the bus and ran toward the woods. The bus driver and passengers sat in awe of the preacher in the woods. After a few minutes, the preacher emerged from the wooded area, running toward the bus while fastening his pants. Upon boarding the bus he shouted to the driver, "Let her roll, Pard! I'm a-feeling fine now!"

Going to most mountain or country churches meant telling what was on your mind. Sometimes it was believed to be divinely inspired, but oftentimes it could make one wonder. Churchgoers gave their "testimony" regularly. It became an outlet to cleanse the soul of troubling things, I suppose. Testimonials, to the churchgoers, could be compared to the opinions of Republicans and Democrats—each had one. However, no one had a testimony like one middle-aged, single woman who desired some male companionship.

It was common for her to give the same testimony night after night. Usually it went like this: "Pray for the Lord to send me a good man." However, one sultry August Sunday night, she began her testimony, "Pray for the Lord to send me a good man." She looked around the congregation, then continued, "I want a man so bad, I get to the bileing [boiling] point!" On this Sunday night, she definitely had a captive audience!

Valley Forge

Baptisms were crowd drawers on Sundays in the country. Some of our church congregations held their baptisms in

Country baptism at Cranberry, North Carolina, 1958

nearby rivers. The church I attended had theirs in a baptistry.

On one particular Sunday morning, the spirit must have filled Big Hazel. No sooner had Brother Buddy, a man short in stature but not in religious stamina, begun singing "Bringing in the Sheaves" than Big Hazel "went up." She was known by the congregation for her obese size, always filling the fourth church pew, literally, and for collecting roots and herbs around White Rock Mountain. She was a large, muscular, weather-beaten woman of few words.

When Big Hazel made it to the front, she had garnered our attention as well as Brother Buddy's. Somehow, we all knew what he must have been thinking. How on earth was he to get a woman of Big Hazel's size submerged in the baptistry? I was glad I didn't have the job. And Deacon Lawrence must have been glad, too. He immediately followed Brother Buddy to help with Big Hazel when they left the sanctuary to go to the baptistry pit.

Sister Wanda led us in four verses of "When the Roll Is Called up Yonder." There was not a sign from Deacon Lawrence as to Brother Buddy's ascent into the baptistry, so as soon as Sister Wanda started "Shall We Gather at the

River," the curtains at the baptistry were slowly opened. There beneath the oil painting of John and Jesus beside the Jordan River was Brother Buddy and Big Hazel.

Brother Buddy was barely visible behind the glass baptistry shield; however, Big Hazel, in her white choir robe, was. She had completely blocked out John and Jesus and took up most of the Jordan River.

Since I was sitting on the third pew, just west of the baptistry, I had what one could term a ringside seat. Brother Buddy said words over Big Hazel, and she made her confession of faith.

The solemn moment was upon us. Brother Buddy had clasped his left hand over Big Hazel's mouth, pinched her nostrils with his thumb, laid Big Hazel back in the water, and then proceeded to lose his footing.

We all witnessed the turmoil going on inside the baptistry pit. Big Hazel and Brother Buddy were under. Big Hazel must have taken her fear out on the water. She became hostile, fighting and kicking to get to the top. Her white robe was clinging to parts unknown to us.

Brother Buddy made it to the top first. He was coughing and sputtering, "Darn it, pull the curtains, Lawrence!"

But before Deacon Lawrence could manage to do so, Big Hazel grabbed Brother Buddy by the nape of the neck with both arms. Brother Buddy had to duck under again to loosen her death grip, but this time he must have done so with a plan. He managed to get behind Big Hazel, and with his shoulder to her sprawling backside, we could hear him grunt, "Heave, Big Hazel, heave!"

Right in the nick of time, too, because Big Hazel must have been on her last breath. She managed to surface right at the baptistry stairwell. The force of her against the stairs made the water splash over and out of the baptistry into the sanctuary.

Deacon Lawrence finally got the curtains starting to close as the Jordan River flooded its banks. Big Hazel was seen wiping her brown, limp, wet hair from her terrified-looking eyes. Her baptism had been a "sight for sore eyes," as my mama used to say. In the painting above the baptistry, John and Jesus were the only two in the church who were the least bit composed and humbled by Big Hazel's baptism. Thank goodness they were there, too, because one had to see it to believe it!

Cranberry

In the fall of 1950, my church was planning their yearly fall revival. The deacon board had heard of a circuit-riding preacher from Johnson City, Tennessee, who could boost large numbers of sinners to the mourner's bench during most revival meetings. They were told, however, he was a more sophisticated preacher from the city.

The deacons were concerned about the behavior of one church member during the revival, Uncle Toby. They feared he would be distracting to the "city preacher" with all his "amens" during his sermon. Uncle Toby always sat in the front pew of the right side of the church where he would be in full view of the preacher in the pulpit. His "amens" would get louder each time he spurted one. Eventually, he would get so wrought up that he would throw in an "Amen, preach it, Brother!" The local congregation had learned to tune him out, but newcomers to the church could hardly hear the preacher for Uncle Toby's "amens."

The deacons invited Uncle Toby to their next meeting. They told him the preacher who was coming to hold the revival was a city preacher and was not accustomed to hearing "amen" shouted from the congregation during the course of his sermon. "He's not used to a lot of commotion in his services," they told Uncle Toby. "Now, Uncle Toby, he's not real formal, even though we have heard he uses notes in his sermon," they told him.

Uncle Toby broke in, "Ain't no man of God if he uses notes. A man of God preaches from the Spirit. You have done got the wrong man. We won't have no kind of good meetin' at all."

They told him the city preacher had a different preaching

style for revivals, and they would all chip in and buy him a new pair of boots if he would promise not to say "amen" during the revival meeting.

Uncle Toby ran his fingers through his thick silver hair and said, "Boys, they say hit's gonna be one of the worst winters ever. Why, the woolly worm's coat is so thick it has to stand up offen the ground to walk! The bark's a lot thicker on the trees, too, this year," Uncle Toby said. "I'll bet it'll snow every day in January, right on up till May, and I shore do need them boots." Uncle Toby hesitated, then said, "I don't know if I can quench the Spirit or not." He then lifted his eyes toward heaven as if to breathe a silent "Forgive me, Lord" prayer and told the deacons they had a deal; he'd not shout "amen."

The week of the revival came. In those days, it seemed the preachers had a set pattern or series of sermons they would preach. The first night, the "backsliders" all came up to the altar after the sermon and rededicated their lives to the Lord again. The second night was dedicated to getting all the neighbors on speaking terms again. This seemed to put to rest any feuding that might have been going on between families during the year. From the third night on, the revival was devoted to getting sinners saved.

Uncle Toby came the first night of the revival and took his regular seat up front. As the sermon progressed, he folded his arms across his chest and began nodding his head up and down in approval. His approval extended into a full rocking back and forth as his silver hair flew wildly all over his head. He did not, however, utter an audible sound even though he was mouthing "amens."

The second night of the revival, Uncle Toby did just like he did the first night, except he crossed his long legs and began swinging his foot up and down as he rocked back and forth mouthing "amens."

The third night of the revival, Uncle Toby started out behaving just as he had the previous two nights. The preacher ardently preached to the sinners, "Now, friends, I'll tell you this. There are those of you sitting right here under the sound of my voice who are going to split hell wide open!"

Uncle Toby had been quiet long enough. He just couldn't stay quiet any longer. He jumped straight up and wildly flung his long arms in sweeping gestures and shouted at the top of his voice, "Amen, Brother! Preach it! Boots or no boots!" The whole congregation had been in on the plan to keep Uncle Toby quiet during the revival. They immediately broke out into laughter, and general pandemonium followed throughout the whole church. The visiting preacher, not knowing what was taking place, asked for the service to conclude with a song and an old-fashioned handshaking fellowship time.

Later, the deacons did chip in and buy Uncle Toby those boots, even though he did not keep all of his promise. I always thought they felt a little guilty and maybe had bad dreams about going to that place the preacher was talking about when Uncle Toby interrupted with his "amen"!

Ollis family picture, 1952
Back left to right: Ray, Lue, Lois, Brownell, Brown. Front: Jean and Joe

The Family Reunion—The Making of Fond Memories

Valley Forge

Family reunions made for many of my best childhood memories. To me, they were wonderful adventures with people I loved, in places I only got to go to infrequently. Food—an abundance of it—was always a drawing card when everything else failed. Aunt Mary's peanut butter-cracker snacks and chocolate fudge, Aunt Nora's triple-layer fresh coconut cake with the warm pineapple filling between each layer, and Aunt Lena's buttermilk-fried crispy chicken worked every time, because kin came from everywhere. The crowds would gather at a respectable site like the Smoky Mountains National Forest, as we did in the '50s, which made for a reunion I will never forget.

My mama, I, and my three sisters, Sonya, Pamela, and Patsy, had to ride with the brave volunteer who opted to transport one widow and three children under ten years of age. This particular year it was Uncle "Speed" from Virginia who had to drive us.

Patience was probably not one of Uncle Speed's virtues. He was a large-framed, stern-faced person who openly stated he wasn't putting up with our foolishness. Immediately it became clear he had not ridden with us before. We were just full of what he wouldn't tolerate—foolishness!

Sonya was five years old, I was seven, Pam was eight, and Patsy was fifteen. We were so contrary with each other that Mama had to draw an imaginary line in the backseat to establish personal boundaries. She would no sooner establish the boundary than one of us would cross it. The whining, complaining, and pinching started. For forty-five minutes, we misbehaved. Mama made threats to kill, abandon, whip-the-blood-out-of, and starve us. Mama knew her game plan was to convince Uncle Speed how she could handle us, but he never bought the idea.

"Lena," he impatiently remarked, "if those kids keep acting like heatherns, you're going to have to do something!"

"Yes, you're exactly right, Speed," said Mama. Her eyes met ours in a manner we had not before seen. We called it the "evil eye."

"Pull over if they even move," she said. We did move, but it was the fifth shrill squeal from Sonya

Jessie's uncle Arthur "Speed" was selected to transport her, her sisters, and her mama to the family reunion.

Family reunion photo at Roan Mountain State Park. Jessie is being held up by her cousin Dwayne Umberger, with brother Sammy, uncle Ernest, and aunt Jenelle.

which pierced Uncle Speed's eardrum. It shattered his nervous system. He swerved the car over to the roadside. Mama had made a threat, and Uncle Speed was meaning for her to carry it out. As the car barely got stopped, Mama leaped from it to get a switch. However, she lost her footing and rolled down an embankment. Immediately we all cleared out of Uncle Speed's car.

Usually, a car pulling from the main Smoky Mountain roadway signaled a black bear had been sighted by a motorist. Bears were frequently seen in the area. Other cars began pulling to the roadside. Voices came from all directions: "Is it a bear?" "Where is the bear?" "Is there a bear down there?"

Among the echoes of voices, Uncle Speed asked where Mama had gone. As Mama pulled herself up the bank by bull grass and tree roots, she met about thirty unfamiliar faces, their eyes fixed on her arrival to the top of the bank.

The first voice Mama heard was a gruff, unrecognizable person. "Is that a bear or not?"

The second voice filtering through the crowd was that of Sonya. "Shucks, no," she said, "that ain't no bear. That's just my Mama!"

Cranberry

The family reunion on my mother's side was usually held at Aunt Flo and Uncle Wiley's house. They had a large country house (the most beautiful one in the area) with lots of acreage, a barn, a spring house, and outbuildings. All of us children loved to explore the barn and buildings whenever we went to Aunt Flo's house. There were tales about the buildings being haunted because Aunt Flo's first husband, who built the buildings, was killed in an automobile accident. The older children delighted in scaring the younger children as we played together. Most of the relatives on my mother's side were from Tennessee, and reunion day was usually the only time during the year we ever saw them.

Ollis family reunion, 1956

There was one elderly aunt and uncle, Aunt Lucinda and Uncle Eli, who attended the reunion every year. Aunt Lucinda was very stern and mean looking. She had very dark, piercing eyes that seemed to stare a hole through you. She never cracked a smile and was always telling my mother and father that they ought to get a handle on us young'uns. Uncle Eli was just the opposite. He was warm, jovial, loving, and always had a twinkle in his eyes. He told us jokes and played jokes on us. We loved him but couldn't abide his hateful wife.

Our older sisters always told us that Aunt Lucinda never wore any underwear. We always rolled and played on the ground around her, hoping to peep under her dress to see if this were true. This technique was to no avail because her dress was always down to her ankles.

Whenever anyone asked Aunt Lucinda how she was doing, she would always answer, "If breathing didn't come natural, I'd be dead. I can barely lift my insides to breathe. I can hardly eat a bite." Yet everyone talked about how her plate was always loaded and looked like it needed sideboards. She would have the children toting second helpings, desserts, and drinks to her constantly! We'd do it, too, in hopes we'd get to the bottom of the underwear question and be the first to tell.

One hot August reunion day, we finally discovered the truth. It was customary to take many pictures at the reunion with the little square black box Kodak cameras. Everyone who owned one brought it for the picture taking. When it came time for Aunt Lucinda and Uncle Eli to sit in the small, straight-back, cane-bottomed kitchen chairs for their picture, two of the children began fighting and were scuffling and rolling on the ground behind the chairs. They "accidentally" pulled over the chair in which Aunt Lucinda was sitting. Those of us who knew what was going on were stationed to get a good view and to size up the matter. Just as the chair toppled backward, Aunt Lucinda's purple dress (she always wore purple) blew up, and there in front of us a rumor proved fact—no underwear!

A highlight of the reunions on my mother's side of the family was the dance which Uncle Verl always did for us. He had lost an arm in World War II and had an artificial one. This intrigued us children. He always showed us how it worked and let us play with it. He would dance by himself while Jean, Lois, and Brownell played "In the Mood" on the

Ollis family gathering, 1960

piano. We all watched with awe. Uncle Verl was kind to all of us children. He always had chewing gum for us and sometimes candy, too! We thought Uncle Verl was the greatest, except when he was tipping the bottle a little too much! Mama would always tell him to go home, that she did not want her children around that stuff or anyone that was drinking it. Uncle Verl always abided by her wishes and would go back to Tennessee.

The reunions on my father's side of the family were much larger than those of my mother's. My father was from a family of ten children. The reunion was held in Cranberry at the "Big House" where I was raised, and it is still held there today. When I was a child, relatives would come for the reunion and stay for days, sometimes even weeks. This reunion, other than Christmas, was always the highlight of the year.

One of the most memorable parts of the reunions was the entertainment. There was always singing, dancing, music making, skits, stories, and individual acts. One favorite cousin, Romina, who was very heavy, would always dance alone most gracefully as the floor shook, and then sing "Lord, Build Me a Cabin in the Corner of Gloryland." Our brother, Bob ("Catman"), always sang and danced like Elvis Presley while the women and girls screamed, swooned, and fell at his feet. Some of the other girls would always imitate our mother and the neighbors in the skits.

At one reunion several years ago, Aunt Nordie was sitting in the living room talking with a large group of relatives. She laid a small, flat hand purse down on the arm of the couch. One of the cousins said to another, "I bet she doesn't have a thing in that purse." The other cousin opened it quickly while Aunt Nordie was engaged in conversation, and the only contents were two tissues. Aunt Nordie always carried that little bag to church and had her tissues for her nose and for wiping tears.

One of the girls left the room and quickly returned. She removed the tissues and inserted panty liners in their place, thinking these might be more absorbent for Aunt Nordie. The cousins laughed until tears ran down their faces, and they wiped them away with Aunt Nordie's tissues! You can imagine the surprise for Aunt Nordie when she opened the small purse in church for her tissues and pulled out a panty liner!

Unlike the Shields family, the Ollis family prided itself for its talents and musical ability. People would come from the small communities around each Fourth of July reunion to hear us sing and watch us perform. We gloried in this and could hardly wait to begin the performances. One summer, Cousin Arbutus from down state in North Carolina came and announced that he and some other cousins had brought some professional entertainers (gospel singers) with them. Cousin Arbutus had arranged all this and said we would have to take up an offering for them to pay for their expenses. When it came time for the singing, they sang for about an hour, and an offering was "lifted." They proceeded to sing for another thirty minutes. All us Ollis brothers and sisters were infuriated because they were horning in on our time and our performance and getting paid for what we so graciously provided free. It looked as if we were not going to get to perform, either.

Many people present were telling our brothers, Joe and Ray, to "put those professional singers on the road" and let our family sing. Joe and Ray did not want to make our cousin from down state mad, so they kept putting off "sending them on their way."

Finally, I walked up to the microphone at the end of a number and announced that the singing would be moved inside and that several had requested the Ollis brothers and sisters sing before they had to leave. We then went inside and started our program. To this day, Cousin Arbutus and his "professional" singers have not returned, and we have not had to share the spotlight with anyone!

Aunts, Uncles, and Other Kin—Better Known as the Family Jewels

Valley Forge

I never did know how so many people were kin to me. My mama was always saying, "Aunt Jenelle's not your blood aunt, but she's just like family." Mama would carefully question every new boyfriend my sisters and I brought home, trying to determine if they were kin to us. I soon learned determining kinship came from respect, kindness, and closeness, as well as blood. Country folks made people feel they belonged even when they didn't.

My Aunt Burnette, who really was a blood aunt, was a family jewel. She had a lovely way about her—everyone was made to feel welcome in her home. She would always take pride in saying, "Come back to see us, 'Nick,' or 'Fred,' or 'Georgia,' or 'Sophie,' or 'Woodrow,' or 'Elvis,'" but herein lay the problem, names. She rarely got one right. She would just call out the first name that popped into her mind. Most everyone who knew her, or about her, knew this. She was such a gracious Southern Lady no one ever seemed to bother to correct her. The "Nick" or "Sophie" went away feeling special, even though he or she was "Nathan" or "Susan," and most always returned.

My Uncle Ernest, a blood relative, was my mother's only brother. Mother said he was "as tight as old Dick's hatband"

and "as tight as the bark on a tree!" He always wore a sport coat, tie (with a genuine diamond tie tack), and dress slacks. He wore a derby-looking hat cocked to the side of his head, which looked swell with his salt-and-pepper hair and neatly trimmed mustache. We called—and I never knew why—Uncle Ernest "Hutch." He could have as easily been called "Scrooge."

I used to ride with him to my Aunt Mary's in Austinville, Virginia. When he came, he would sort of "pop in," have a bite to eat, sleep over, and "pop out." At our house, with three children under ten years of age and two teenagers, Uncle Hutch never stayed for long. Mama was glad when Uncle Hutch would "pop out" to another relative's house because he usually took one of us with him, and I was usually the one who would go along.

Uncle Hutch left our house with a full stomach. He made another stop at Aunt Mary's in Austinville. Over the years, I was a regular passenger in Uncle Hutch's 1957 Oldsmobile, which always ended up at my Aunt Mary's, where I was unloaded.

If I got thirsty or needed a necessity break along the way to her house, Uncle Hutch always headed for a Virginia rest stop. I knew all of them. He would stop, then say, "Let's take

Uncle "Hutch"

a necessity break. Don't forget to get a sip of that good cold water (from the outside fountain), it's free!"

I believe Uncle Hutch lived in fear I'd ask him for a "pop." Mama warned me before every trip, "Ask for a soda, and it'll be your last trip."

I can never remember Uncle Hutch getting more than twenty-five cents worth of gas. Many times he carried along lady friends who seemed to "pick up the tab." I liked it when they came along, because they always made him exit at an Esso or Phillips 66 service station. When one of his misses was along, Essos and Phillips 66s meant a pack of nabs and a Grapette for me—talk about living! I tried to take teensy-weensy bites to make my nabs last until I got to Wytheville. Every now and then I'd get greedy and put a whole nab in my mouth. I quit doing that the day I nearly choked to death between Chilhowie and Marion, Virginia. I figured Uncle Hutch would have left me for dead beside U.S. Highway 11. He wouldn't have wasted money on a hospital visit. I can never remember his having to go to the hospital until he died at age ninety-one. Uncle Hutch's moderate and frugal lifestyle has endeared him in my memory.

Cranberry

Then there was my Uncle Wiley who came to eat Sunday dinner with us as sure as Sunday rolled around. Mama would be in the kitchen getting dinner ready, and I would be in the living room pestering Uncle Wiley to give me a nickel. (If Mama had only known how I pestered him for that nickel, she would have spanked me good or, as she put it, "set my fields on fire"!) Sometimes Uncle Wiley would "come across" with that nickel, depending on his mood, I suppose. His frequent bywords were "Ah, you take...." When he began a sentence with "Ah, you take...," I knew I would not get a nickel that Sunday. He would say, "Ah, you take, you don't need no nickel today. I gave you one last Sunday!" As he got older, I got the nickels more frequently, because he would forget from one Sunday to the next if he had given me one the previous Sunday! My mama never knew about the nickels, and I was the richer for it!

My aunt Liz was a heavyset mountain woman who walked very slowly with a slight limp. She always dragged a crutch behind her, supposedly to aid her in walking, but never seemed to use it. Aunt Liz was a good-humored, warmhearted person who loved children. She was dark skinned with dark eyes and a wrinkled face and white hair that was swept back away from her face and wrapped around a "rat." She always wore an apron and gave the appearance of a hardworking woman. She dearly loved to argue a point and did so in her own good time.

Aunt Liz lived next door to me with three of her grown children and her mother, my great aunt Lessie. My uncle had died years earlier. Aunt Liz came to my house every morning, as soon as daylight would break in the sky, to get a quart of milk to make gravy for her family for breakfast. Around 6:30 a.m., she would bang her crutch against the floor and doors, then make her way through the living room and bedrooms to our kitchen, awakening most of us as she went. She loved to discuss the 6:00 morning news with Mama while Mama got our breakfast. Daddy always called her the "A.P." (Associated Press); he called another one of our neighbors the "U.P." (United Press). She was a talker, too.

One morning Aunt Liz remarked to Mama, "This world has gone to the dogs! I heard an old song this morning on the radio that said, 'Oh, my butt's got a hole in it'!" Mama told her the name of the song was "Oh, My Bucket's Got a Hole in It." Aunt Liz didn't buy Mama's clarifying the name of the song, so she said, "I knowed what it said, and it said what I told you it did. My hearing is still good!"

After hearing what Aunt Liz said to my mama, I thought that my daddy had a right to call her "A.P." I was sick and tired of her waking us up so early to gossip, and could've thought of a lot worse names to have called her. I wouldn't have said them aloud, because I would have gotten the switch from Mama. But a girl has a right to think them, doesn't she?

My great aunt Lessie would sometimes go to Pop's General Merchandise herself to get a tin of Bruton's Dental Sweet Snuff if she missed making connection with my sisters or me to get it for her. She always carried her snuff and a birch twig for dipping the snuff everywhere she went. We purposely tried to miss seeing her because we would play her organ while she was gone to the store for the snuff.

Aunt Lessie had a beautiful old pump organ in her bedroom, but she wouldn't let us girls see it or play it. Whenever we saw her going down the road to the store to get her snuff, we would run up to Aunt Liz's, and she would open Aunt Lessie's bedroom door. Aunt Lessie always locked it when she left. One of us girls would be playing the organ, and the others would watch for Aunt Lessie to come around the big curve in the road. When we spied her coming, we would run home before she came and caught us playing her organ.

Favorite topics of discussion at Pop's General Merchandise were the birth of new babies and who was going to have the next baby in the community. One particular day at the store, it was announced that a woman in the community had just had her thirteenth child that morning. Someone around the stove asked how much the baby weighed, and the conversation turned to the birth of premature babies.

At this point, Great Aunt Lessie (who, by the way, was ninety-one years old at this time) spoke up and said, "They tell me that when I was barned [born], you could set a tea cup over my head and the rim of it would rest on my shoulders."

One of the old-timers around the stove looked at her intently and asked, "Well, did you live?"

Great Aunt Lessie replied, "They said I did, and done well!"

My aunt Pansy could definitely be classified as a family jewel. She was a barrel of laughs. She had a keen sense of humor, and we never lacked for entertainment when she was around us. She was married to my daddy's brother.

I remember one winter Saturday when two of my sisters and I went to see her. "How are you, Aunt Pansy," we asked when she came to the door.

"Children, I'm just about dead," she replied. "I haven't been out of the house all winter."

Interestingly enough, I had seen her walking down the street in front of her house the week before. As we entered the living room, I noticed she was dressed completely with red high heel shoes, rouge, lipstick, and powder. I saw her coat draped over the back of the chair by the door, and I knew Aunt Pansy was getting ready to go somewhere just as we arrived!

"What's been wrong, Aunt Pansy?" we asked. "Have you been sick?"

"Children, I've been just about dead ever since I got run over by a car in Elk Park the other day," she replied.

Not having heard of her misfortune, we asked her what happened. She proceeded to tell us she had accidentally stepped in front of a car as it was pulling away from the side of the road. She said the driver was looking the other way and had not seen her. She was knocked down in the street and had spent three days in the hospital recuperating from bruises, contusions, and a sprained arm. She told us her doctor had told her she ought to look into getting hit by the car, because she might make money from it. Aunt Pansy thought the doctor meant she should make it a practice of getting hit by cars just for the money.

She said, "You think about that doctor wanting me to go out and get hit by cars for money! I told him I wouldn't be run over like that again for a million dollars!"

Aunt Pansy was the official heat thermostat adjuster at our church in the winter. She made it a practice to go to the back of the church toward the end of the service, pull up the door in the floor, and go down the steps to the basement to turn the heat off.

For some reason, she just could not wait until church dismissed. One church night, she tip-toed up the steps after turning off the heat just as the preacher was dismissing the service. She carefully tried to close the trap door during the prayer. All of a sudden, just when the preacher prayed, "Lord, let us feel your presence this week," Aunt Pansy dropped the door. Bang! Everyone jumped and began to scream, and, of course, that was the end of the preacher's dismissal prayer. It didn't seem to bother Aunt Pansy one bit. She just looked around the church and said, "Well, children, I drapped that thing!"

Aunt Pansy told us about her brother's recent marriage at age seventy-eight. She said he had been "sparking" a widow woman who was seventy-six. The woman had a grown son who knew his mother was seeing Aunt Pansy's brother. Her brother had gone to see the widow lady one day and said to her, "Let's get married." Aunt Pansy said the widow lady said, "Well, let's!" They immediately went to the courthouse, got their license, and got married all that same afternoon.

Later that evening, around 9:00, the married couple went to bed. Aunt Pansy said, "You know, they just went to bed together like married folks will do!"

A knock came on the bedroom door, and it was the widow lady's son. When he saw them in the bed together, he said, "Mom, I never thought I'd see the day you would go to bed with a man right under my nose."

Aunt Pansy said, "My brother just propped up on his elbow in the bed and told him to look over there on that dresser at that piece of paper and he would see why they were in bed together."

The son went to the dresser and picked up the marriage certificate, read it, and laid it back on the table. He then walked over to the bed and put out his hand to Aunt Pansy's brother and said, "Hello, Dad!"

We all enjoyed being with Aunt Pansy. She had a way of making us feel special. When you were with her, there was never a dull moment!

Schooling and the Like—Learnin' and Actin'

The schools we attended in the '50s were merely an extension of our home life. I loved and respected most of my early elementary school teachers just like I did my parents. I also knew the wrath of their punishment if I misbehaved. I not only got disciplined at school, I got the same thing again at home when my parents found out about my conduct at school.

Jessie's relatives in the early 1900s in front of school

Cranberry

Sweeping the floor, cleaning desks, and washing black-boards were common chores for students who worked for their lunch. When Elk Park Elementary School got a lunch-room, it was a dream come true for the community. The lunchroom was built down on the big play area below the school, which sat upon the hill. There were several tiers of wooden stairs descending the steep hill to the lunchroom. Inside, the manager and her helper, along with girls in the seventh and eighth grades who worked for their lunch, waited to serve the students. The food was delicious!

In those days, students could take produce to trade for lunch tickets. We rode to school on the "cracker box" bus dri-ven by Mr. Harve Turbyfill, better known as Uncle Harve. The bus had a bench seat along each side and a split bench seat in the middle. This middle bench had an opening under it. There, during the harvest season, could be found bags of potatoes, corn, cabbage, green beans, and other produce to be traded for lunch tickets. Sometimes we would take pota-toes to trade, but it usually took everything we raised to feed our large family of eleven including Mama and Daddy.

It was common year-round to find sacks of shelled corn on the bus to be taken to the grist mill to be ground into corn-meal. Students were allowed to take the corn down to the mill during the morning recess and get it ground into corn-meal, then go back during the afternoon recess and get it. The mill was located just at the bottom of the hill from the school. Travel was difficult in those days, as few people owned automobiles. The school bus served a multiple pur-pose, just as the mail truck had.

Uncle Harve, the bus driver, was a kind and understand-ing man. He loved all the students and tried to help and advise us. Some of the older boys in Cranberry, such as Hobie, a seventh grader, did not want to go to school when they got in the seventh and eighth grades. Almost every morning Hobie's father would bring him to the bus stop and wait with him until Uncle Harve came. Uncle Harve made sure he did not get off at any stop before getting to school. However, when Hobie got off the bus at the school, he would go straight down the hill and head back home. Of course, his father would go off to work thinking he had gotten Hobie off to school one more time!

Our parents modeled for us a hearty work ethic. They always told us we could do anything and have anything we wanted if we were willing to get an education and work hard. We worked at school for our lunch and to pay our "book fees." We would sweep the room during recess while the other students were playing. This was a chore. It was most difficult to sweep under the stationary desks with the folded seats which were bolted to two strips of wood running the length of the room. My brother Bob occasionally helped the janitor sweep the halls. He liked to do this because it was easy. The janitor would put a sawdust-like compound on the oiled wood floors, after which Bob would push a large brush broom down the halls. One year Bob's and my job was to clean the boys' and girls' bathrooms. Bob did the boys', and I did the girls' bathroom. He complained constantly about that job, but he did it, just as I did. The best job was working in the school store during recess and after lunch. All my sisters and I eventually had this job. It was a pleasant job because I had the chance to see my friends and all the students in the school who came to buy ice cream.

Some of my fondest memories of elementary school are of Mr. Wally Brown, the principal. Mr. Brown had a tremendous influence in the lives of many students. He taught us to have values, convictions, and standards and to be true to them. He started the Literacy Club and taught those of us in the club to appreciate fine literature. We had to read books and give book reports. We were required to commit poetry to memory and to deliver it on club meeting days. To this day, I can still recite most of the poetry I learned. Mr. Brown taught a woodworking class to eighth graders. I took that class and made a milking stool to use when I milked the cow. I still have the stool. I later padded and covered it to use as a foot stool.

The county health nurse used to come to the school to check the students for head lice and the itch. My sister Ludella told about the time the nurse came and asked as she checked Mary, a little blonde girl, if she had any lice. Mary answered with a broad smile and a twinkle in her beautiful blue eyes, "Yeah, just a few." Everyone had to lay their heads on the desk for this examination, and when it was over, they had to lay their hands on the desk and spread their fingers so the nurse could examine for the itch. If lice or the itch was found, a note was sent home telling the parent what to do. Usually, the remedy for the lice was putting kerosene on the hair to kill the nits. The itch remedy was a paste of sulphur and lard.

The only thing that could smell worse than itch remedy was ramps, a form of wild onion. In the spring, when ramps were in season, some students would come to school reeking with the odor. Sometimes some of the boys would slip them in and rub them on the radiators so we would get to go to the library while all the windows were raised and the room was aired. If ramps were eaten by the student body, school had to be dismissed. The smell of eaten ramps on a human body could be nauseating to a non-eater of ramps. Boy, did we eat the ramps!

Speaking of radiators, one of my sisters told about the time a student wet her panties and the teacher washed them and put them on the radiator to dry. Was she ever embarrassed! Today, I guess a teacher could be brought before the highest court in the land for such an act!

My sixth grade teacher did more for my self-esteem by writing in my yearbook, "Love and Admiration, Mrs. Hampton." I didn't know what the word admiration meant. As fast as my feet would carry me when I got off the school bus that day, I ran for the only dictionary we had in the house and looked up the meaning of admiration: "To regard with wonder and delighted approval. To have a high opinion of."

She thinks I'm wonderful, I thought. *She looks up to me. I amaze her. She likes what I do in class.*

All these thoughts raced through my mind. From that day

forward, I was determined to "make it" in school. I worked hard, studied late at night, and worked diligently on my schoolwork. I graduated valedictorian of my high school class. Thank you, Mrs. Hampton. I'm sure you never knew how you touched my life! Even though you're gone...Love and Admiration, Jean.

Valley Forge

School musicals were one of the few times parents and kin came to visit the school in number. Our school gym doubled for a social arena. The gym was the site for PTA meetings, Watkins' rallies, Scouts, recitals, 4-H, Christian Bible Ministry (you could read the Bible and pray together back then), and musicals.

At Valley Forge School, musicals were practiced from almost the start of school. You could see the teachers' relief when they'd come up with, "This year's musical theme will be...!" Relief, relief! The best musical, of sorts, I can remember was one which centered around the American Indians. We even had an Indian musical star—Hiawatha. The girls all got to try out for the part, if we wanted. I didn't because I couldn't carry a tune in a paper sack, and it was a genetic flaw for my sisters and brother, too. Hiawatha was out for us. But not for my friend Connie. Even though Connie was a grade behind me, I always considered her my best friend. She was dying for the star's role—leading lady so to speak. I wanted her to have it, too, and she could have gotten it if it hadn't been for a natural songbird who moved into the parsonage that year, Natty Nurse.

Natty was a Hiawatha type, sparkling large brown eyes, long chestnut colored hair, and a presence about her like royalty. She had captured the hearts of all the fifth, sixth, and seventh grade boys on her first day of school. My friend Connie and I saw her for what we knew she would become—the leading lady, Hiawatha.

The big night came. The gym was packed. The teachers

were stressed but hopeful. This was to be the musical of all musicals, all because of the preacher's daughter, Natty Nurse. For openers, Natty was to come onto the stage where a tepee sat. She was to sing her rendition of an Indian maiden's song as she walked toward the heartthrob of the school, Tommy Coates, who was in the role of chief. Tommy (the chief) and Natty (Hiawatha) were to catch hands, sing a duet, and go down the cinder-block-and-board-constructed steps and onto the gym floor, where the rest of us kids were sitting in threes behind poster board facades of canoes. Tommy and Natty would then get into their own canoe as we all sang (or mouthed, in my case) another Indian ditty. The teachers had practiced us tirelessly and continuously to have us all row in sync, then row off with the chief and Hiawatha into the sunset.

Well, that was how it was to be in our musical, but it didn't happen. What happened was this: Natty Nurse came onto the stage face to face with our own gorgeous Tommy Coates. All eyes, including Tommy's, were on her. We waited and waited—nothing. Natty was caught in the worst-case scenario for a leading lady—stage fright. My friend Connie knew every word and was Natty's back-up. Mrs. Knip immediately jerked Natty off and put my best friend in the whole world, Connie, on as Hiawatha. I thought she did Hiawatha well. It didn't even matter to me about her red hair and freckled nose either. I thought it gave Hiawatha character. I was elated, since Natty was out and Connie was in. It happened so fast, some of the lesser of us Indians had missed the switch, and even if we saw it, we didn't understand about a new leading lady stand-in. Mrs. Knip hadn't mentioned it. Curiosity was piqued. We did what all curious Indians in a musical would do, we stared instead of doing our lines.

When Tommy (the chief) and Connie (the new Hiawatha) came down the steps and onto the gym floor, we sat in our canoes just gazing. Mrs. Knip's face took on a dark hue of red. She finally got us from our trance, and we got back on the musical track. I managed to get a "thumbs-up" to my friend Connie, and just as she was "thumbs-upping" to me,

Tommy Coates hit his canoe, and it toppled over. He and Hiawatha had to sit on the floor and pull the canoe front up and lean it against their right arms while they faked paddling with their lefts. We all managed to row our canoes into the sunset as Mrs. Hadden, our other teacher, moved her flashlight, the improvised sun, across the black poster board sky.

The audience must have loved us, mistakes and all. They clapped and "bravoed" enthusiastically. It was the night a star was born, my best friend, Connie. Natty Nurse got put in her place; however, we knew her popularity wouldn't be hurt, because she now was liked by all the girls, who "felt sorry for her," as well as the boys. I think everything went great, because I heard Mrs. Knip say, "This is one we'll remember!"

Cranberry

My third grade year at Elk Park Elementary School was the first year I was introduced to the theater via school plays. We performed the operetta *Madame Butterfly* for all our parents, friends, relatives, and the rest of the school body. Every girl in the third grade wanted the role of Madame Butterfly—after all, she was the star of the play. We all knew who would get the lead part. None other than Madame Butterfly herself, Junie. She was a feisty little girl who flitted around from one group of girlfriends to another and delighted in trying to keep us all mad at each other. She was a master at this, even in the third grade! But she was a natural butterfly. We all knew she would get the part. Sure enough, she did.

The play was written for Madame Butterfly to emerge from her cocoon as a beautiful butterfly. A song was to be sung as all of the other butterflies gathered around her in a tight circle to hide her while she changed from her cocoon costume to a butterfly costume. We had practiced it to perfection. However, all the girls had other ideas on the night of the play. When the time came for the butterflies to gather around Madame Butterfly for the metamorphosis, we all gathered at arms length around her with our legs spread apart so Junie could be easily seen in her nakedness from outside the circle.

From behind the curtain, Mrs. Nester, our third grade teacher, was whispering to us, "Bunch up, bunch up, hide her." We all pretended not to hear her. Madame Cocoon/Butterfly was devastated. She didn't know what to do! Finally, Mrs. Nester reached an arm through the curtain and pulled Junie from the circle behind the curtain. She helped Junie change into her butterfly costume and pushed her back through the curtain into the circle. The play went on, but we had accomplished our task. For the first time, we had all ganged up on Junie, plotted against her, and won! No more running from girl to girl trying to keep us mad at each other all the time. We had Junie's number. However, Mrs. Nester had our number. For the next two weeks, all the third grade girls except Junie had to stay in the room at recess and sweep the floor, clean the desks, and wash the blackboard. We didn't care. We took a stand and made our point. Junie soon learned her little schemes and plotting were no longer going to work on us. We finally did accept her as one of us after her mother came to school and gave us a Christmas party complete with balloons and cake!

School musicals were, indeed, an integral part of our schooling. The fifth grade school musical was a Mother Goose play with the lead character being a little girl in a garden singing "I'm Forever Blowing Bubbles." In each bubble, there was the reflection of a Mother Goose character who was woven into the story. I tried for the leading part for singing and reciting. I was chosen. I was elated! My joy soon diminished as I learned each student had to bring $2.50 for his or her costume. Our mother always made our costumes from a scrap of cloth or something when we were in a play, but this time one lady was going to purchase the material and sew all the costumes. My family had no way to raise $2.50 for the costume. Finally, I had to tell the music teacher, Mrs. Wooten, and my teacher, Mrs. Wise, that I did not have the $2.50 to pay for the costume. Mrs. Wooten, the music teacher, said she was sorry but that her daughter, Charlotte, who was in the sixth grade could do the part. She said Charlotte had practiced all of it with her at home because, unbeknownst to anyone else, the music teacher had chosen her daughter as the stand-in for the lead part in the play. It was very difficult that day for me to sit back and watch Charlotte rehearse my role because I did not have $2.50 for the costume material.

When we went back to class, and the afternoon recess bell rang, my classmate, Johnny Ray Goode, asked Mrs. Wise if he could make an announcement. Johnny Ray said he did not want Charlotte for the role in the play, and he asked my classmates if they would bring a nickel or dime the next day to help pay for my costume. They did. I did get to be the leading lady, thanks to my dear friends, especially Johnny Ray. Mountain children had a way of taking care of each other in time of need. This proved to be one of those special times.

Jean with brothers Joe and Bob (behind), 1950

Passing Away—Laying Out the Dead

In Cranberry, Mama was the nurse, the doctor, the veterinarian, and the undertaker for the whole community in my early childhood years. We never knew when someone was going to come running to our house wanting Mama to go with them to see about a sick relative, a sick cow, or to "lay out" the dead. Mama would just drop what she was doing and give us instructions to carry on at home, and off she would go to help in any way she could.

I remember one time when she was called upon to come to the aid of a choking cow. The cow had been eating apples, and one had gotten stuck in its throat. After a few minutes of trying to figure what to do, Mama could see the cow was going to choke to death. She finally just rammed her hand and arm down the cow's throat and got the apple before the cow knew what was happening to it. Afterward, it made weird sounds, coughing and carrying on, but my mama saved that cow, and it was never forgotten by us.

Mama would stay up for nights with a sick child or adult, if needed. She just had that knack for caring for the sick and helping during a crisis. I guess that's why there were many in my large family who entered the medical profession—everything from medical secretaries to medical record administrators, nurses, dentists, and doctors.

When Mama would "lay out" the dead (which meant preparing them for burial), she would then come back home and send us around the neighborhood to tell everyone of the death. She would instruct us to tell the women to cook plenty of food to take to the home of the deceased. Someone always brought a banana pudding (you could count on it); thus, it became known as "funeral pudding." When I was small, funeral pudding was (and still is) one of my favorite desserts. I couldn't wait to get to the home of the deceased to get some of that good banana pudding. I would always get some of my aunt Nelle's because her pudding was definitely the most pleasing to my palate!

I didn't relish having to go through the living room where the corpse would be laid out. It always gave me the creeps. I was frantically afraid of a corpse as a child. My great aunt Lessie had told us ghost stories of corpses "burping" when someone would go by them at night as they were laid out in their casket before burial. Of course, Mama tried to console me by telling me the stories weren't true. I wanted to believe her, but at night when I was in bed, I'd have nightmares about the "burping corpse." It would take me weeks to get back to normal after a death in the community. Mama would always say, "Jeannie, it's not the dead you should be afraid of. It's the living."

I remember when one particular man died (everyone called him "Pap"), his family marvelled at how good looking he was as a corpse. Pap always wore bibbed overalls, seven days a week. On Sunday, he would put on a white shirt with his overalls. When he died, someone in the community bought him a suit in which to be buried. When we all went to the house to see him after he was "laid out," his family had put him upright in the corner of the room and had taken pictures of him in his suit. They said, "Ain't Pap pretty?" and "Ain't he the naturalest looking human being you've ever seen?"

Well, yes, we all did think Pap looked pretty good. I just hated he was already dead and didn't get to join in on the fun of seeing how good he looked himself!

At Pap's funeral, his son stood in the middle of the service and went to the front of the church. He requested that my mama's girls sing over Pap. We all looked at each other, not quite knowing what to do.

The preacher said, "Since it has been requested by the family for you girls to sing, we'll just have your number right now. Come on up."

We stood, went to the front, and tried to think what song we could sing. Just as I sat down at the piano, another family member requested we sing "The Unclouded Day." I began to play the song. We knew one verse by heart, so we just sang the same verse twice and sat back down. From that point on, we tried to be prepared to sing at funerals if we were asked. We often were, and we were better prepared after having to sing unprepared over Pap!

A few years later Pap's wife, "Mam," died. Right away her son came to the house and told Mama he wanted her girls to sing over "Mam" just like they did "Pap." At least we had fair warning, and of course we carried out his request.

Funeral homes became popular in the late '40s to the Cranberry and Valley Forge natives. The newest funeral homes were located in Newland and Elizabethton. The days of someone in the community preparing the dead for burial were soon gone. My sisters and I sang for many funerals. We were such frequent singers that we became well acquainted with the funeral directors.

I remember when we were singing at one particular funeral how emotional the family became during the course of the service. In those days, at the end of the funeral service everyone in the church would proceed single file by the casket and look at the corpse one last time. We would always have to sing a song during this time, and a funeral director would stand at each end of the casket as the people walked by for the final corpse viewing.

During this time, one family member became unusually distraught. He practically pulled the corpse from the casket. The casket began to shake and move. The two funeral directors began to hold on to each end of the casket. I could see the funeral director at the foot of the casket from my position at the piano. He had large black eyes that became bigger and bigger by the minute with the shaking of the corpse.

The funeral director was holding to the casket so hard, it looked as if rigor mortis had even set in on him! Finally, the preacher came from behind the pulpit and got the family member to lay the corpse back down, after which I watched the color slowly return to the undertaker's face. It was all we girls could do to keep our composure and continue singing "Nearer My God to Thee" during the ordeal! Years later, we saw the undertaker and reminded him of the incident. He said that was one funeral he had never forgotten!

When Great Aunt Lessie died, her grave marker had her age listed as ninety-four years, ten months, and two days. When her good friend Lockie Jane saw this, she said it was wrong. She said Aunt Lessie had always lied about her age and she was 105 if she was a day old.

When the local men dug Aunt Lessie's grave, someone misjudged the width, and it was much wider than the standard grave. A grass mat covered the grave and the rack the casket was placed upon. One of the pallbearers, Wendell Dugger, was a local young man known for being scared of his shadow, but always trying to appear to be very brave.

As the pallbearers were carrying Aunt Lessie's casket to the grave site, Wendell cut the corner to set the casket down on the rack before lowering it into the grave. He stepped on the grass mat with no ground under it and fell completely into the grave! The stern old funeral director known as Doc Sims hid behind a tombstone and tried to muffle his sounds as he shook with laughter. He remarked to the other funeral director that Wendell came out of the grave faster than he went in!

Funerals in the country were occasions for measuring the status of the deceased, as well as that of the relatives left behind. The number of people attending the funeral was taken into account as well as the number of those who called at the home and signed the funeral registry. Neighbors talked for days about "who took it the hardest." This was determined by the one who screamed and cried the loudest and then "passed out" or "fainted away." The floral offerings were counted, and remarks were always made about whose spray or basket of flowers cost the most.

Flower girls were used to carry the flowers from the church to the hearse and flower van. It was considered a great honor to be listed in the paper and in the funeral registry as a flower girl or a pallbearer.

My sister Lois told me about one funeral in which she was a flower girl. The cemetery was just in back of the church. There was a downpour of rain all day. It did not let up for the funeral. One of the funeral directors asked Lois if she would take some of the flowers on over to the grave site instead of taking them all into the church for the funeral service. Lois replied she was sure that would be fine with the family; however, it was not. When the family arrived and discovered all the flowers were not in the church, they demanded that they be brought back. The funeral director complied. Both he and the flowers were soaked. The funeral director had not brought any more racks for displaying the flowers, so they were propped, dripping wet, on the front pew so the crowd could count them!

One of my most vivid memories of growing up in Cranberry was the annual cleaning off of the cemetery in preparation for Decoration Day held the third Sunday in August. In my early childhood, there was not any perpetual routine care of the cemetery as there is today. The men of the community met on a designated Saturday morning prior to Decoration Day to mow the briars, cut the grass, fill in sunken graves with dirt, and generally prepare the cemetery so people could find the graves and walk around easily to place flowers on them. The ladies of the community would prepare a picnic lunch and carry it to the cemetery on clean-up day. One year, at the picnic, Uncle Clarence tasted iced tea for the first time. He drank so much of the new drink that he couldn't work much that afternoon for going to the woods to "step to himself." Entire families took part in this annual event. It was a joyful gathering with food, fun, work, and fellowship enjoyed by all.

Funerals were judged by how well ministers conducted the service. There usually were two or three ministers who participated in the service. One conducted the obituary, one prayed, and the other one tried to bring an evangelistic service by scaring all who were not "saved" into repentance and salvation before their appointed hour of death came. Most families did not prefer this, but it was a given for most country funerals anyway.

My sister-in-law Glenna told about her aunt Tissy, who had told the preacher how she wanted her funeral conducted. She told him to read the fourteenth chapter of John and say a few words. The preacher asked her what three songs she wanted sung. She said she always liked "Rock of Ages" and "Amazing Grace."

He said, "Tell me one more song you would like to have sung when you die, Aunt Tissy."

Aunt Tissy thought and thought. She finally said, "Oh, I don't know, just surprise me!"

Ollis funeral gathering for Jean and Grace's father, Brown Ollis

PHOTO ALBUM

Jessie's Grandmother Pearman and her family in early 1900s

Jessie's Grandfather
Emmet Pearman

Jessie's aunt Nora and uncle Ernest (Hutch) as children in the early 1900s.

Jessie's relatives on her father Samuel Shields's side of the family (late 1800s). Note: The deceased family member still made the photograph in the framed portrait.

A country homeplace of Jessie's grandparents in the early 1900s.

Family reunion time at Rhododendron Gardens on Roan Mountain, Tennessee. Jessie with Aunt Jenelle Merryman and Aunt Jessie Brooks White.

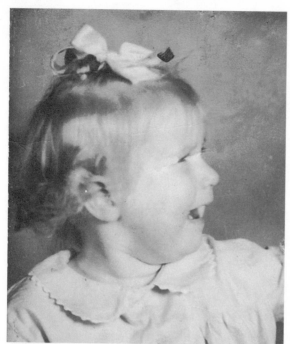

Jean Ollis Honeycutt
on April 1, 1945.
First photograph.

The Ollis sisters, (front) Jean, Lue, Brownell, (back) Lois, and Grace.

Christmas in Valley Forge in 1953. Santa brought dolls for Sonya, Pam, and Jessie.

Jean Ollis Honeycutt (left) and Grace Ollis Calhoun with mother, Bertha, on the Cranberry homeplace front porch, 1950.

CONCLUSION

Growing Up Country and Liking It! was aimed at jogging another country-bred person into remembering how times were back then. It was also written to let citified people know what they missed if their childhood was different. Most of all, it was written to put a smile on the face of the reader.

Growing up in the Appalachian Mountains was a humbling experience whether it was in Western North Carolina or Northeast Tennessee. No one had much wealth in the way of money, but we were blessed with the riches of family, which meant love, togetherness, cooperation, steadfastness, hard work, and kindness. The Southern Appalachians provided a backdrop of beauty for a life enriched with daily experiences—whether good or bad. These experiences were builders of character—a good sense of humor flourished....

"As happy a man for as any in the world,
For the whole world seems to smile on me."
—Samuel Pepys

Growing Up Country was truly a memorable experience for the three authors. We appreciate your sharing our memories.